Lois Lowry

My Favorite Writer

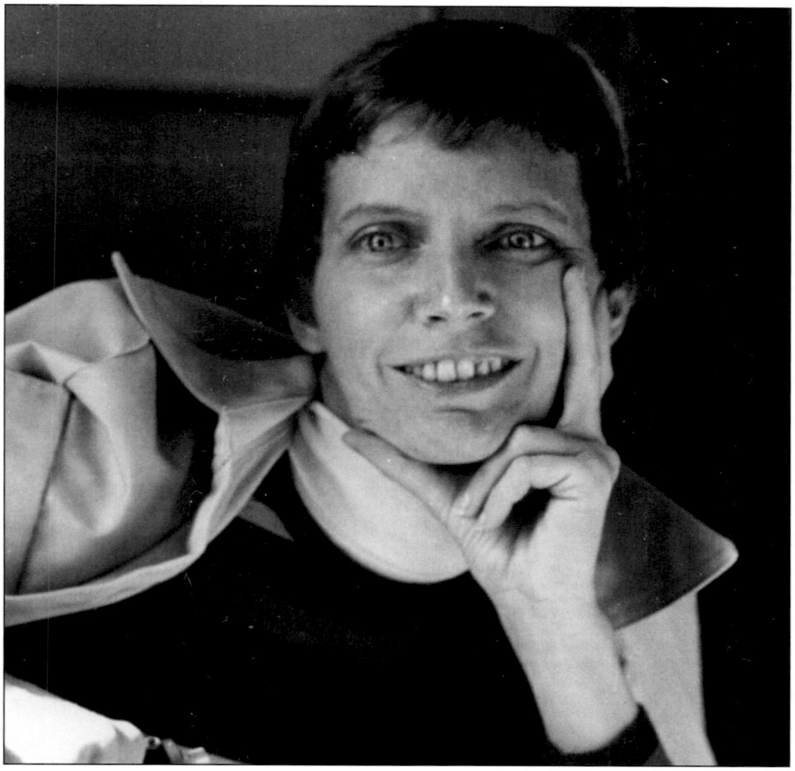

Lily Erlic

WEIGL PUBLISHERS INC.

Published by Weigl Publishers Inc.
350 5th Avenue, Suite 3304, PMB 6G
New York, NY 10118-0069
USA
Web site: www.weigl.com

Library of Congress Cataloging-in-Publication Data

Erlic, Lily.
Lois Lowry / Lily Erlic.
p. cm. -- (My favorite writer)
Includes index.
ISBN 1-59036-286-1 (hard cover : alk. paper) -- ISBN 1-59036-292-6 (soft cover : alk. paper)
1. Lowry, Lois--Juvenile literature. 2. Authors, American--20th century--Biography--Juvenile literature. 3. Creative writing--Juvenile literature. I. Title. II. Series.
PS3562.O923Z65 2006
813'.54--dc22

2004029928

Printed in the United States of America
1 2 3 4 5 6 7 8 9 0 09 08 07 06 05

Project Coordinator
Tina Schwartzenberger

Substantive Editor
Frances Purslow

Design
Terry Paulhus

Layout
Jeff Brown

Photo Researcher
Kim Winiski

Contents

Lois Lowry

MILESTONES

1937 Born March 20, on Oahu, Hawai'i

1948 Lives in Japan and learns about Japanese **culture**

1950 Moves to New York City

1956 Marries Donald Lowry, a naval officer

1977 Her first book, *A Summer to Die*, published the same year her marriage ends

1990 Wins the Newbery Medal for her novel, *Number the Stars*

1994 Wins the Newbery Medal for her book, *The Giver*

2000 *Gathering Blue*, a **companion** book to *The Giver*, published

2004 *Messenger* published

Millions of people read Lois Lowry's books. **Settings** in her books are descriptive, vivid, and clear. Some characters in Lois's books are based on herself or people that she has known.

Her first book, *A Summer to Die*, is loosely based on the life of Lois's sister. In the story, sisters Meg and Molly do not get along. Eventually, they begin to become friends. Then Molly learns that she has a disease called leukemia. She soon dies. *A Summer to Die* is a sad story. *Number the Stars*, another book by Lois Lowry, won an award called the Newbery Medal. The book tells of a friendship between two girls and how they help a family escape from the Germans during World War II. *The Giver*, another Newbery Medal winner, is a novel about a boy living in a **futuristic** society.

The **themes** in Lois's books are about human relationships. Her characters show friendship, courage, love, and hope. Lois writes from her heart.

Early Childhood

Lois Lowry has traveled to and lived in many places. She was born on Oahu, Hawai'i, on March 20, 1937. Her family had a house in the town of Waianae. Lois was the middle child. She had an older sister, Helen, and a younger brother, Jon. Lois's father, Robert Hammersberg, was an army dentist. Her mother, Katherine Landis, was a homemaker.

Lois learned to read when she was 3 years old. Her mother and father encouraged her to read. Her mother read books to Lois. Lois's father told stories of his youth.

In 1941, Pearl Harbor, Hawai'i, was bombed. Lois's father had to leave the family. He served on a hospital ship during World War II. He eventually went to Japan. Lois spent these years with her brother, sister, mother, and grandparents in her mother's hometown, Carlisle, Pennsylvania. Her grandfather often read her poems. She spent many of her childhood days at the public library. Lois knew that she would become a writer one day.

"Nothing 'inspired' me to be an author. It was simply what I always wanted to do, from childhood, what I did best, loved best. If anything inspired me, it was books."
Lois Lowry

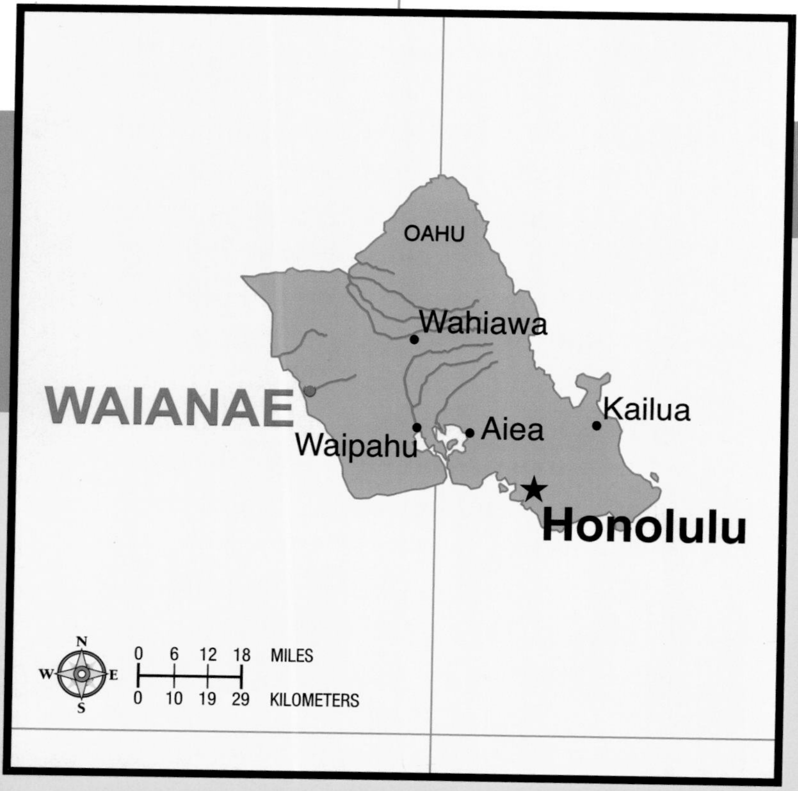

When Lois was born, Waianae was a small town on the island of Oahu. Today, the city attracts many tourists.

At school, Lois was very advanced in reading and writing. She skipped grade 2. At first, Lois enjoyed grade 3. One day, she received a multiplication assignment. Lois did not even know how to add and subtract. Multiplication terrified her. Lois suffered from what she called "math anxiety" throughout school. Still, her love of reading was much greater than her fear of math.

Lois was a shy, quiet child. She would rather spend time with a good book than playing with friends. Lois's reading was like training for when she became a writer. She learned about language and how stories develop. Lois's **vocabulary** increased. She could put words on paper and create wonderful stories.

Helen is 3 years older than Lois. Their brother, Jon, was born when Lois was 6 years old.

Growing Up

Lois's father remained in Japan after World War II ended. In 1948, Lois and her family moved to Japan to be reunited with him. Lois and her family lived with other American families in a community called Washington Heights. They lived in different types of houses, ate different types of food, and wore different clothes than the Japanese. The community had its own church, movie theater, library, and elementary school.

Sometimes, Lois snuck out of the community. She rode her bicycle down the street to observe Japanese life. Lois ate Japanese foods with her friends.

Lois and her sister attended Meguro School in Japan. They learned many new things about Japanese culture.

Lois and her family lived with other American families in a community called Washington Heights.

For holidays and special occasions, Lois sometimes dressed in traditional Japanese clothing, including this kimono.

By the time Lois was 12 years old, she had lived in 3 American states and 2 countries.

Lois loved Japan. The years she lived there influenced her writing. Although Lois has never written about her experiences living in Tokyo, she remembers it helped her learn about cultural differences. The Japanese way of life was different from her own. Lois learned about the geography of Japan, as well. Lois would never have developed a sense of how other cultures live if she had stayed in a small town in the United States.

Inspired to Write

Lois Lowry created an imaginary world. As a child, she **mimicked** characters in the books that she read. The playacting helped her create her own characters when she began writing.

Meiji Shrine is the largest shrine in Tokyo. The shrine is in Yoyogi Park, in Shibuya. Shibuya was one of Lois's favorite places to explore in Tokyo.

"In blue jeans and sneakers (at 12 years of age), with my best friend from junior high, I explore my way comfortably around the huge, sprawling, noisy, crowded city (Tokyo) by bike and bus and train without a qualm."
Lois Lowry

Often Lois explored the area called Shibuya in Tokyo. She describes what she saw, "It is crowded with shops and people and theaters and street vendors and the day-to-day bustle of Japanese life." Lois remembers the smells of charcoal and fish fertilizers, and the sounds of music, wooden sticks, and wooden **geta**. Lois recalls the schoolchildren dressed in dark blue uniforms.

In 1950, the Korean conflict began. American women and children were evacuated from Japan. Lois and her family returned to her grandparents' home in Carlisle, Pennsylvania. In 1951, the family moved to Governors Island in New York City.

Lois's father gave her a typewriter for her thirteenth birthday. She appreciated this generous gift. She used the typewriter in high school and college.

As a young girl, Lois loved the excitement and bright colors of Tokyo's Shibuya district. Shibuya is one of the most popular shopping and entertainment districts in Tokyo.

In high school, Lois won a national award for student writing. She then attended Pembroke College, the women's branch of Brown University, located in Rhode Island. Lois enjoyed college. Her English professor told her she wrote well, but lacked life experience. Lois thought otherwise. She felt she had many experiences to share.

After 2 years of college, Lois left school. She married a naval officer named Donald Grey Lowry in 1956. Lois was 19, and her husband was 21. The couple moved to San Diego, California, where Donald was stationed. Together, they had four children. Alix was born in Connecticut in 1958. Grey was born in Florida in 1959. Kristin was born in 1961, and Benjamin was born in 1962. Both children were born in Massachusetts.

While living in Cambridge, Massachusetts, Lois learned that her sister, Helen, was dying of cancer. Lois wanted to travel to Washington, DC, to visit Helen. Sadly, Helen died in 1962 before Lois could make the trip. Years later, Lois wrote about the emotional experience in her first novel, *A Summer to Die.*

Lois married Donald Lowry in Washington, DC.

Favorite Authors

When Lois was 8 or 9 years old, her mother read her *The Yearling* by Marjorie Kinnan Rawlings. This book changed her life. Lois read the 400-page book again to herself. She knew she wanted to become a writer. *The Yearling* won a Pulitzer Prize for literature and became a classic. The book is about a young boy and his fawn in the backwoods of Cross Creek, Florida. Lois's other favorite books were *The Secret Garden, My Friend Flicka,* and *A Tree Grows in Brooklyn.*

Learning the Craft

When Lois was an adult and her children were attending school, she decided to return to school. Lois attended the University of Southern Maine. She received a bachelor of arts degree in 1972, the same year that Alix graduated from high school. Lois went to **graduate school**, studying photography and literature.

Lois fulfilled a childhood dream when she began writing in the 1970s. At first, she wrote stories for newspapers and magazines. Lois wrote simple stories that reflected her own life. Then, a children's book **editor** from a publishing company called Houghton Mifflin read Lois's stories. The editor asked if Lois would like to write for children. Lois said she would. Instead of completing graduate school, Lois decided to finish writing her first book. When she was 59 years old, the University of Southern Maine gave Lois an **honorary degree**.

Lois fulfilled a childhood dream when she began writing in the 1970s.

Lois's earliest publications were English textbooks.

In 1976, Lois finished writing *A Summer to Die*. The novel was published the following year. Although the book is fiction, it is also somewhat **autobiographical**. The story is about the death of a young girl and how it affects her family. Many of Lois's books are about making connections with others.

Lois creates characters before she begins writing a story. She imagines her characters as real people. In Lois's imagination, they have names and faces. She can also hear them speaking. When Lois has a good sense of who her characters are and how they act, she sets a series of events in motion. This is how she writes her stories.

Lois's marriage ended in 1977, the same year her first book was published. Two years later, she moved from Maine to Boston, Massachusetts. In 1980, she met a man named Martin, with whom she shares her life. Together, they have six grown children and nine grandchildren.

Inspired to Write

Lois Lowry has helped many new writers learn to write better. She believes that reading is the key to learning to write well. She says her own writing improved because she read many books. Lois recommends writing letters to a friend or grandparent to practice writing. The letters should be written as though telling a story.

Lois and Martin divide their time between their homes in Maine and Massachusetts.

Getting Published

> "I love the process of putting words on a page, rearranging them, making them work somehow, hearing them slip into a sequence that sounds right...."
> Lois Lowry

Before writing her first novel, Lois wrote stories for magazines. She wrote stories about children for adults. Lois wrote about herself and her family. She wrote about life after World War II.

Lois's novel, *Number the Stars,* won the Newbery Medal in 1990. The award is very respected. Winning the award helped Lois become successful. *Number the Stars* is based on a true story. Lois's friend, Annelise Platt, was a child in Denmark during World War II. Annelise told Lois about the horrors of war. Annelise described cold homes during winter. She talked about how her sister died during childbirth because no professional medical care was available. Lois wrote Annelise's story for children.

The Publishing Process

Publishing companies receive hundreds of **manuscripts** from authors each year. Only a few manuscripts become books. Publishers must be sure that a manuscript will sell many copies. As a result, publishers reject most of the manuscripts they receive.

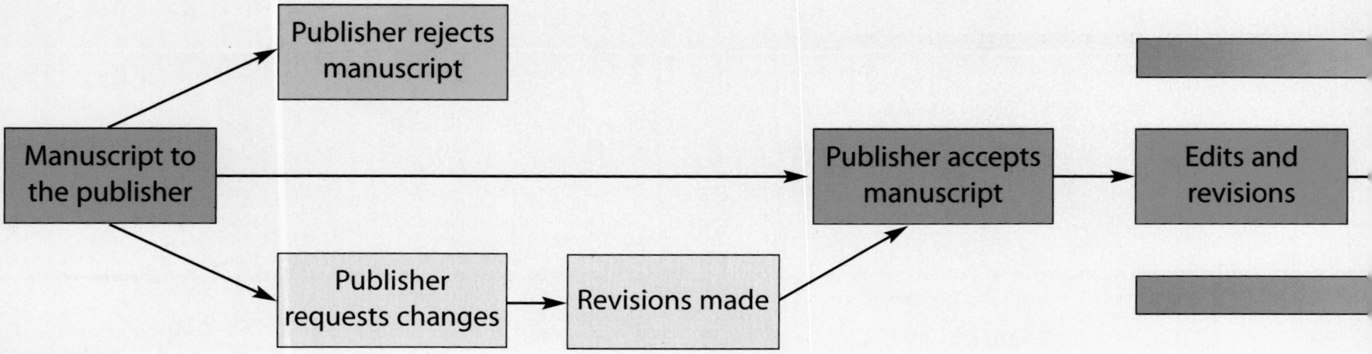

Lois **submitted** her work to a publisher called Bantam Doubleday Dell Books for Young Readers. They published the book. Many people asked Lois to speak at schools about *Number the Stars*. Children all over the world read the book, which was translated into twenty languages.

The Giver also won the Newbery Medal. Although the book was well written, some parents objected to it. These parents did not want their children to read about a **totalitarian** society. Lois is pleased that the book creates discussions in classrooms all over the world. Lois has since written two more books, *Gathering Blue* and *Messenger*, that have some of the same characters as *The Giver*. These three books are considered a **trilogy**.

Inspired to Write

Lois's life experiences and her love of dogs have influenced her writing. Children often ask Lois, "How do you get your ideas?" She tells children that the ideas come from her life. For example, the idea for *Anastasia, Absolutely* came to Lois one day when she was walking her dog.

Once a manuscript has been accepted, it goes through many stages before it is published. Often, authors change their work to follow an editor's suggestions. Once the book is published, some authors receive royalties. This is money based on book sales.

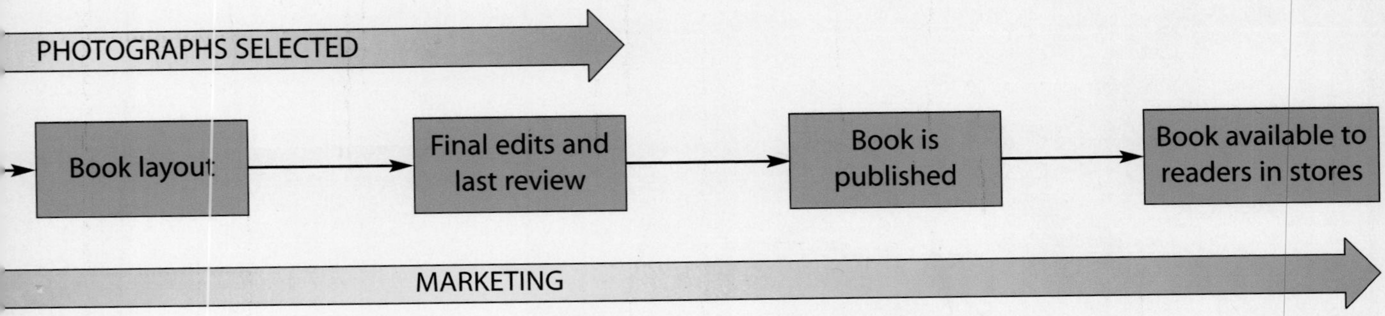

Writer Today

Lois Lowry continues to write. She writes for nearly five hours each weekday. Every day, Lois sits at her desk. She completes *The New York Times* crossword puzzle. Lois listens to classical music and drinks coffee while she writes. Her books show her love of writing and her sense of humor.

Recently, Lois and Martin bought an old farmhouse in Maine, closer to their grandchildren. Mountains, lakes, and wildlife surround the house. Sometimes wild turkeys look into the house through the windows. Bandit, their Tibetan terrier, lives with them, too. Lois reads, gardens, and entertains, as well. Their other house is in Cambridge, Massachusetts. In this house, Lois has original paintings on the wall, given to her by **illustrator** friends. Bookshelves full of books fill most rooms in the house.

Lois says that she is embarrassed to show people her office in Cambridge, Massachusetts. She feels it is disorganized.

Writing has helped Lois through difficult times. Whenever something painful or unhappy happened in her life, she wrote. Lois's son, Grey, became a fighter pilot. He died in 1995. Lois misses him terribly. Grey's death was a sad time for Lois, but her family and her writing gave her comfort.

Lois has given speeches at many conventions and conferences. Teachers and librarians attend to hear Lois speak. She talks about her books and their meaning. Lois also tells the audiences about her life.

Lois had two sons, Ben and Grey.

Popular Books

Lois Lowry enjoys writing for children. She has written for adults, but Lois is best known for her novels for children and young adults. She writes about historical fiction, science fiction, and fantasy.

Number the Stars

In *Number the Stars*, Lois writes a story of friendship and courage. She tells of a close friendship between two girls and a caring family who help others. Ten-year-old Annemarie Johansen lives in Denmark in 1943, during World War II. The Germans **occupy** Denmark. Annemarie's best friend is Ellen Rosen. Ellen is Jewish. She must hide in Annemarie's house, away from the German soldiers. The soldiers are trying to evacuate all the Jewish people from Denmark. Annemarie's family wants to help their friends the Rosens. Soon, the family realizes that Ellen is no longer safe with them. Annemarie helps her friend and others escape to the safety of Sweden.

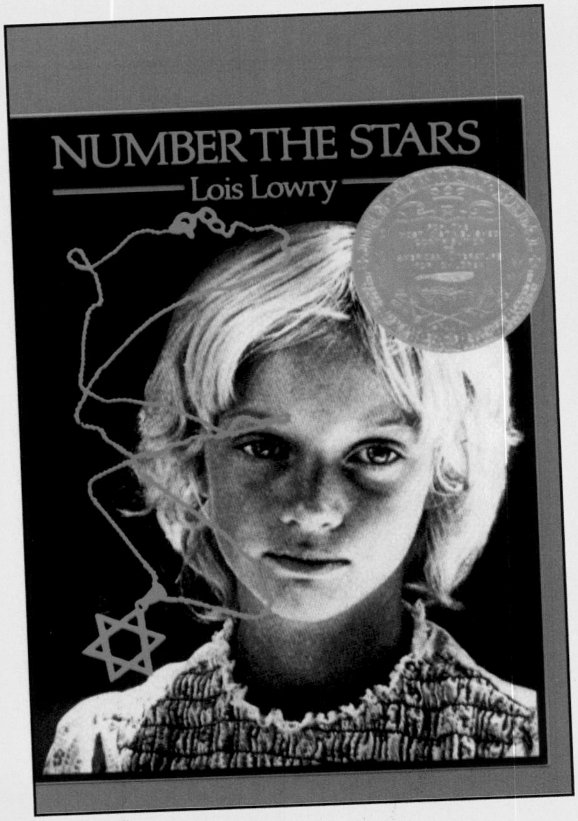

AWARDS

Number the Stars

1989 Sydney Taylor Award

1989 School Library Journal, Best Books of the Year

1990 Newbery Medal

1990 National Jewish Book Award

1990 Booklist Editor's Choice

1990 ALA Notable Book for Children

1990 Wisconsin Golden Archer Award

1991 Maine Student Book Award

1991 Wyoming Indian Paintbrush Book Award

1992 New York Charlotte Award

The Giver

The Giver is one of Lois Lowry's most popular books. Many middle school and high school children in classrooms all over the world read this book. In *The Giver*, Lois creates a society with different rules. In this futuristic story, the main character is a boy named Jonas. In his community, no one can make choices. The Committee of Elders makes decisions for everyone. The rest of the community follows the rules set out for them. Jonas's society has no disease or crime. The people have no memories. One day, the Committee of Elders decides to make Jonas the receiver of memories. Jonas receives all the memories of history, war, pain, snow, and colors. Along with the memories, he also receives wisdom to make choices. He chooses to leave the community. Jonas sets out to create a new future because he realizes his community is not as perfect as he thought it was. Jonas experiences many new things outside the community.

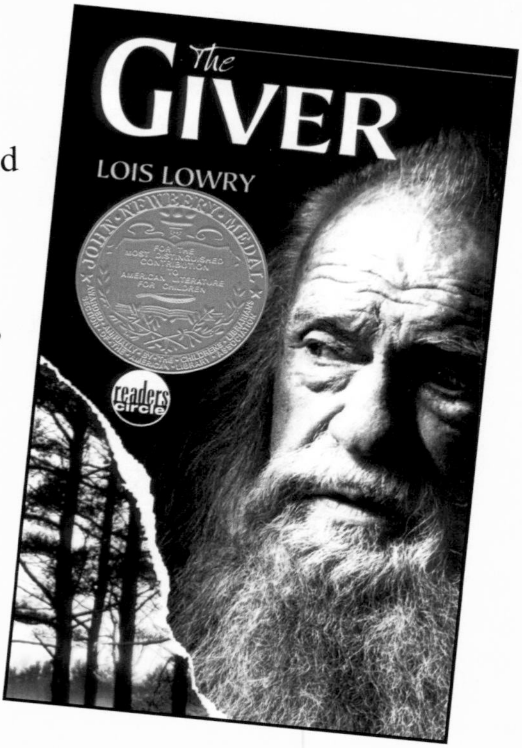

AWARDS
The Giver

1993 School Library Journal, Best Books of the Year

1993 Boston Globe-Horn Book Award

1994 Newbery Medal

1995 Arizona Young Reader's Award

1995 Maine Student Book Award

1995 Pennsylvania Young Reader's Choice Award

1995 Maryland Black-Eyed Susan Book Award

1996 New Jersey Garden State Teen Book Award

1997 Ohio Buckeye Children's Book Award

AWARDS
Anastasia Krupnik

1979 Parent's Choice Gold Award

1983 Michigan Young Reader's Award

Anastasia Krupnik

Anastasia Krupnik is a funny story. It is the first book in a series of books about Anastasia Krupnik. Anastasia is a 10-year-old girl. She writes her thoughts and makes a list in her green notebook. On her list, she writes everything she hates and everything she likes. Her parents tell her that they are going to have a baby. She places "parents" and "babies" on her hate list. Anastasia Krupnik will make readers laugh out loud.

AWARDS
Anastasia, Absolutely

1997 Iowa Children's Choice Award

1998 Garden State Children's Book Award Nominee

1998-99 Hoosier Award Nominee

Anastasia, Absolutely

In *Anastasia, Absolutely*, Anastasia is in grade 8. Anastasia has a dog, which she walks every morning before school. One morning, she makes a big mistake. Anastasia's mother asks her to mail some drawings to her publisher. Instead of putting her mother's drawings in the mailbox, she drops the bag she used to pick up after her dog into the mailbox. Read this book to learn how Anastasia tries to correct her mistake.

All About Sam

Sam is Anastasia Krupnik's lovable younger brother. He has appeared as a character in many Anastasia books. This story covers Sam's life from the time he is a newborn until he is a toddler. Sam takes readers on many adventures. He has his own ideas about haircuts, nursery school, and eating broccoli.

Gooney Bird Greene

Gooney Bird Greene, a second grader, arrives at Waterford Elementary School wearing pajamas and cowboy boots. Her classmates decide that they want to hear Gooney Bird Greene's story at story time. The teacher allows Gooney Bird to tell stories to the class. The stories are creative and exaggerated. Gooney Bird enjoys being the center of attention. Every day, she tells a **far-fetched** story. One story is called, "How Gooney Bird Came from China on a Flying Carpet." The story is actually true. Gooney Bird came from a town called China. She was rolled up inside a carpet, which flew out of the car. Gooney Bird's classmates enjoyed listening to her tales. You will, too!

By the Two-Time Newbery Award Winner
Lois Lowry
GOONEY BIRD GREENE

AWARDS
All About Sam

1988 School Library Journal, Best Books of the Year

1991 Mississippi Mark Twain Book Award

1991 South Dakota Prairie Pasque Award

1991 Arkansas Charlie May Simon Children's Book Award

1992 California Young Reader's Medal

1992 Georgia's Children's Book Award

AWARDS
Gooney Bird Greene

2002 Parents' Choice Silver Award

2002 New York Public Library-100 Titles for Reading and Sharing

Creative Writing Tips

Lois Lowry worked hard to become a good writer. She studied writing at university, where she **honed** her writing skills. Here are some tips that may help you improve your writing.

"READING is the most productive thing for me, I think. If I read brilliant paragraphs I want to rush out and write brilliant paragraphs."
Lois Lowry

Reading

Most writers read a great deal. They visit libraries and bookstores. Exploring books helps writers improve their writing. Ask your teacher, librarian, or bookseller for suggestions about which books to read. Read a wide range of authors, and eventually you will develop your own style of writing.

Take Writing Courses

There are many writing courses available for children and young adults. A community or recreation center may offer courses on journaling or creative writing. Lois took many courses in writing through college and university. Taking a course will help you practice so that you can learn to write well.

Lois has received many awards for her books, including the 2004 Massachusetts Book Award for *The Silent Boy*.

Find Your Own Space

Most writers have a special place where they write. Lois Lowry writes in an office in her home. Find your own space where you can write. Perhaps it is a corner of a room or a desk. Keep your notepads, pens, or computer at your special writing spot. Having your own area is important. It will help you concentrate on your writing.

Rewrite

After a writer completes a first **draft** of the story, he or she makes changes. Rewriting makes the story better. Some writers finish the first draft, put it away, and then read it again a few days later. This allows the writer to think about the story. Lois Lowry rewrites until she is happy with her words. Then Lois sends the story to her publisher. Most times the publisher will ask Lois to make more changes.

Inspired to Write

Lois Lowry creates stories in her mind before she writes them down. She can see the beginning and ending of the story. Lois's memories of her life experiences have been woven into fiction. She takes events that happened in her own life and shapes them into stories.

Lois and Martin's house in Maine was built in 1768.

Writing a Biography Review

A biography is an account of an individual's life that is written by another person. Some people's lives are very interesting. In school, you may be asked to write a biography review. The first thing to do when writing a biography review is to decide whom you would like to learn about. Your school library or community library will have a large selection of biographies from which to choose.

Are you interested in an author, a sports figure, an inventor, a movie star, or a president? Finding the right book is your first task. Whether you choose to write your review on a biography of Lois Lowry or another person, the task will be similar.

Begin your review by writing the title of the book, the author, and the person featured in the book. Then, start writing about the main events in the person's life. Include such things as where the person grew up and what his or her childhood was like. You will want to add details about the person's adult life, such as whether he or she married or had children. Next, write about what you think makes this person special. What kinds of experiences influenced this individual? For instance, did he or she grow up in unusual circumstances? Was the person determined to accomplish a goal? Include any details that surprised you.

A concept web is a useful research tool. Use the concept web on the right to begin researching your biography review.

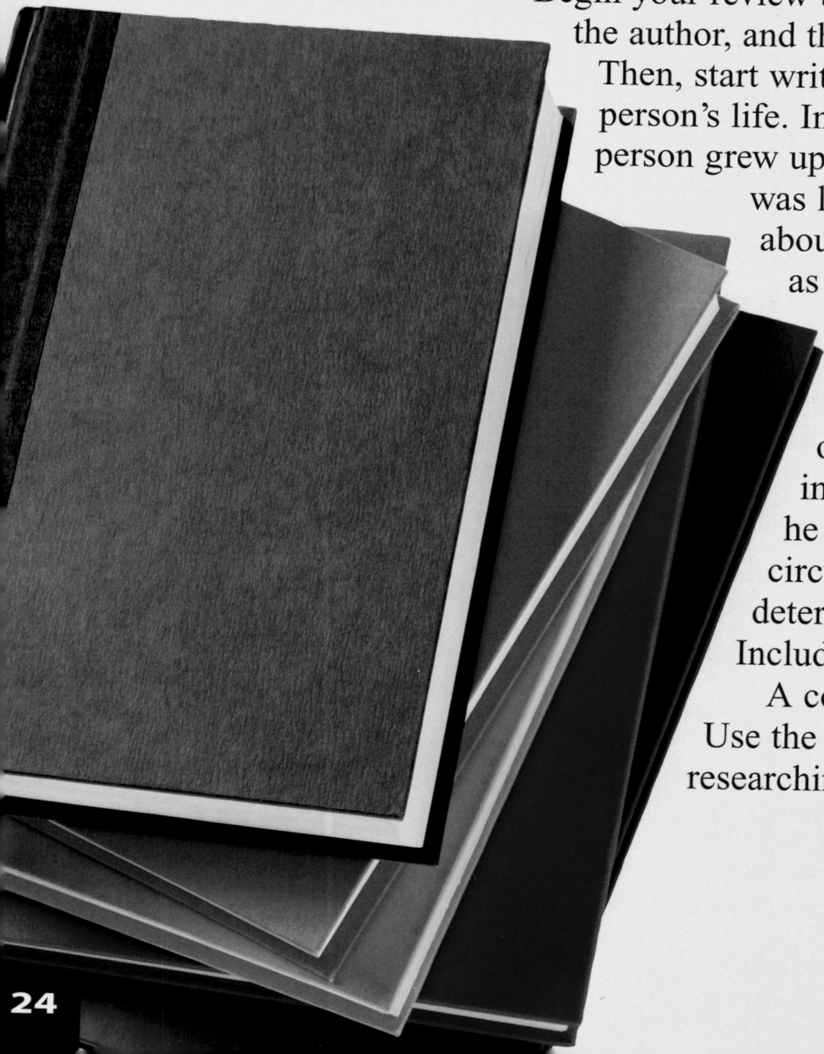

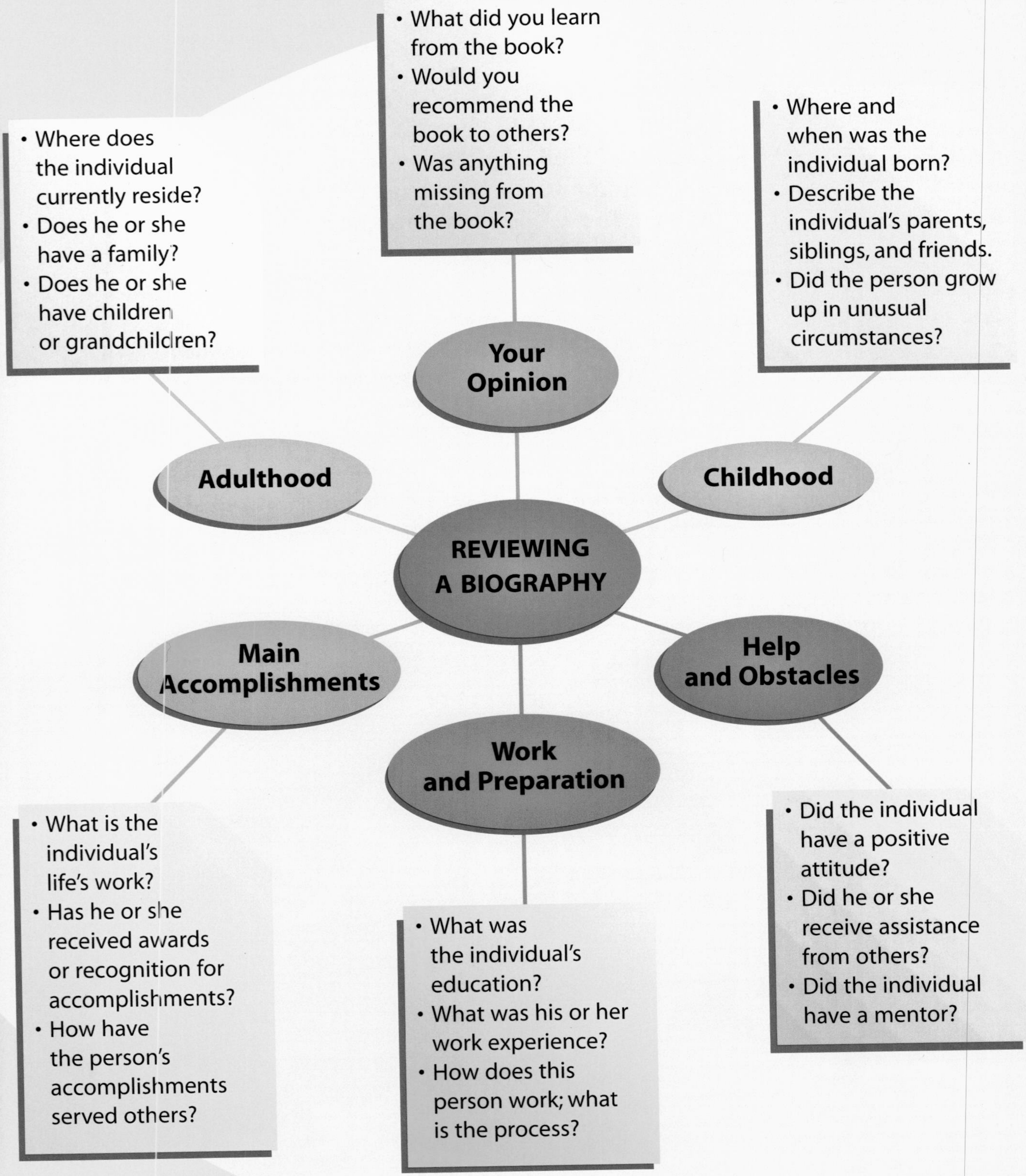
REVIEWING A BIOGRAPHY
Your Opinion
• What did you learn from the book?
• Would you recommend the book to others?
• Was anything missing from the book?
Childhood
• Where and when was the individual born?
• Describe the individual's parents, siblings, and friends.
• Did the person grow up in unusual circumstances?
Help and Obstacles
• Did the individual have a positive attitude?
• Did he or she receive assistance from others?
• Did the individual have a mentor?
Work and Preparation
• What was the individual's education?
• What was his or her work experience?
• How does this person work; what is the process?
Main Accomplishments
• What is the individual's life's work?
• Has he or she received awards or recognition for accomplishments?
• How have the person's accomplishments served others?
Adulthood
• Where does the individual currently reside?
• Does he or she have a family?
• Does he or she have children or grandchildren?

Fan Information

If you want to know more about Lois Lowry, you should read a book that Lois wrote called *Looking Back*. The book is full of pictures and memories from Lois's life. *Looking Back* tells how many of these experiences became stories. In the book, Lois also answers many questions her fans have asked.

After Lois wrote *The Giver*, many fans wrote her e-mails and letters asking about the ending. They wanted to know more about what happened to the main character, Jonas. Lois wrote two more companion books to satisfy her curious readers.

Many of Lois's books have been translated into different languages. Her books are popular in classrooms all over the United States, as well. Lois's books have **stimulated** student's minds and promoted discussions across the country.

Lois attends conferences and book signings to meet her fans.

Lois has an interesting Web site for fans who want to learn more about her life and her work. On her site, Lois answers frequently asked questions. She tells her fans that she will continue writing more Anastasia and Sam books because she never tires of writing about the Krupnik family.

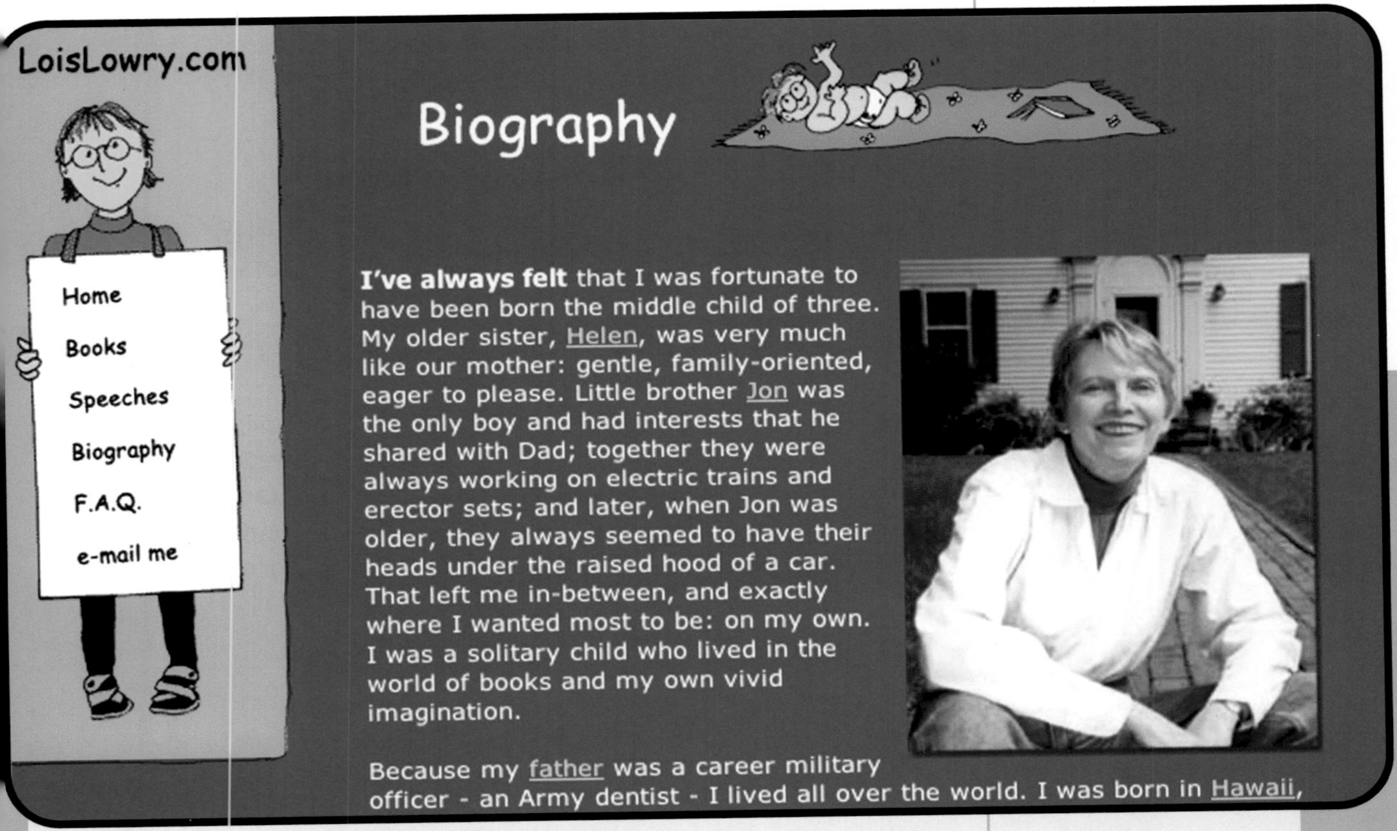

LoisLowry.com
Biography
Home
Books
Speeches
Biography
F.A.Q.
e-mail me
I've always felt that I was fortunate to have been born the middle child of three. My older sister, Helen, was very much like our mother: gentle, family-oriented, eager to please. Little brother Jon was the only boy and had interests that he shared with Dad; together they were always working on electric trains and erector sets; and later, when Jon was older, they always seemed to have their heads under the raised hood of a car. That left me in-between, and exactly where I wanted most to be: on my own. I was a solitary child who lived in the world of books and my own vivid imagination.
Because my father was a career military officer - an Army dentist - I lived all over the world. I was born in Hawaii,

WEB LINKS

Lois Lowry

www.loislowry.com

This Web site gives fans insight into Lois's life. Her biography and books can be viewed here. Fans can also read speeches she has given at conferences.

Author Study: Lois Lowry

http://www.carolhurst.com/authors/llowry.html

On this Web site, visitors can read about Lois and some of her books.

Quiz

1

Q: Where was Lois Lowry born?

A: Lois Lowry was born in Oahu, Hawai'i.

2

Q: Does Lois have any brothers or sisters?

A: Yes. Lois has a younger brother named Jon. Her older sister, Helen, died of cancer.

3

Q: What country did Lois live in when she was 11 to 13 years of age?

A: Japan